THE TENDEREST PETAL HEARS

Charlotte Renk

THE TENDEREST PETAL HEARS

Charlotte Renk

Blue Horse Press
PO Box 7000 – 148 Redondo Beach, CA 90277
2014

Copyright 2014 by Charlotte Renk

Cover art: Jen Floyd

Editors: Jeffrey Alfier and Tobi Cogswell

ISBN-13 978-0692243619

The ear is only a petal that grows from the heart. When we hear…
it all becomes a garden.

The Book of Awakening, Mark Nepo

DEDICATION

To my three children, Claire, who writes as well, and who loves science and admires my work (occasionally weeping at poems that touch her deeply). She has accompanied me at numerous readings and workshops all over the state. Victoria, and Chet, who also write poetry, fiction and non-fiction, support my efforts. They have sacrificed time that we might have shared, but they understood the importance of what I do. To Al Cook, PhD., who listens to my work almost daily and who lovingly supports my efforts in so many ways, from listening to my poems to responding with praise and suggestions. To Edith, my long-time friend and fan, who read and helped me select the poems to be included in this book. And finally, to one special Poet-friend who believes in my writing and who urges and encourages me to do it, despite the many domestic and emotional demands on my energy.

Table of Contents

Part I: World Yowls and Riffs

Utmost Aftermath of Terminals, Cats, and Song	1
That Thumb in My Chest	3
Ubiquitous Voices of Boot, Panties, And…	4
Punctuating Adrian	6
Lament for a Common Day	8

Part II: Psyche Admonishes and Murmurs

Witness	12
Leaky Pen Whimpering in Sonora	14
Komodo Dragon Meets Swollen Red Palm	15
Erosion Sighs and Cornbread Whines	17
Sweet Surrender	19
Seventy-Nine Days	21

Part III: Past Echoes

Synesthesia of Crystal's *Summer Time* Blues	24

The Way of Cows	26
Unclasping Alice	27
Mama Rasps *Help* as Queen of the Night Inherits	29
Nonc Jules and Lachez-Les	31
Not Sure Why I'm Confiding	33
Spoonful of Vanity; Year Full of Vision	35

Part IV: Woods Whisper

Restless Heart Hears and Asks	38
To Bark, Who Speaks a Handful	39
"A Bird in the Hand…"	41
Just a Dove's Worth	42
So *Confused,* Said the Squirrel	44
Spotted Bee Balm Soothes Parched Pasture	45
Acknowledgments	47
About the Author	48

PART I. WORLD YOWLS AND RIFFS

Utmost Aftermath of Terminals, Cats, and Song

Finally home, I'm exhausted, numb, sleepless.
Though fed, Greedy Gut whines, meows, yowls
outside while Cornbread curls and purrs beside me.

As he sleeps, my head streams voices of ice, airports
and canceled flights. Sky Link's flat robotic tone warns
me to step away from the door (automatic, oblivious)
and to hold onto the bar before the shuttle bolts
then scuttles and slings me to Terminal B.

Another faceless imperative advises us not
to leave bags unattended, lest confiscated, searched.
Arrested? for Wright's *Country Music*, Silber's *Fools*?

A child in a stall says *Stop, You're hurting me.*

A stoic Airway Rep repeats: *Sorry, no vouchers…*

No flights for two more days…Sorry…Sorry, Ma'am.
Try Gate B-12, and she stalks away. On my way
to B-12 (*a vitamin?)* I stop for solace—*food.*
Vendor asks: *$7.34. For Gardetto's and Mountain Dew?*
I fume, rummage, and clutch my bag for security.

I am not my thoughts, I say to myself, trying to stop
the thawing faucet of thoughts from flooding
frustration of last 3 days.
 "Resistance breeds persistence…Breathe deeply."

Frozen, faceless voices echo terminal to terminal...

*Mama's terminal...couldn't even remember how to slip on her slippers, how to peel a banana, how to swallow **it**, much less the life she's known.*

And Orbison's song sings itself over and over:
I thought that I was over you, but it's true, oh so true, that when I saw you last night....
Then Carol King chimes in:
Will you still love me tomorrow?

Mama's dying, and tomorrow's gone.
All I want now is to go home, really home
to Eleuthera's* pink sands, clear waters.

Smart folk dream more, I'm told,
but if cold, we're prone to nightmare.
Tonight, Aaron Burr and I shall duel again,
and he'll kill me for sure.
My feet are sore and cold, and my head hurts.
Greedy Gut still yowls at my door.

*Originally Greek word meaning Freedom; small, sickle-shaped island of Bahamas

That Thumb in My Chest

Mr. Purusa, the little thumb in my heart,*
takes the blue velour easy chair, legs lifted,
arms folded, face grinning yellow as my walls.
He listens and watches commotion in this room
of Victorian décor—doilies, wallpaper jasmine
flanking the west window where heavy drapes
block last afternoon sun.

And he says nothing, does nothing except sigh
and thumble around as he sits there in my chair
amid all that scrambling, slamming, grabbing
cans from the cupboard, pots to the stove
as thoughts race, replay the ways and whys
of what was said and what wasn't. Meanwhile,
feelings reel from the hurry-ups, the musts,
the can'ts, the wants, the don't wants.

And if that's not enough, the evening news
reports more casualties and more threats as
two loudmouths rant and banter hardball politics
about implications of the bombing and the heat.
And I'm sweating as I scurry to get supper and
kids grouse about homework and *needing* the car.

Sometimes, I can see him there, Mr. Purusa,
just sitting silently, bewildered and sad about
all that mental static. I'll bet if he could,
he'd like to jump out of my muttering mind,
climb onto the knobs of my TV like a...like a...
tiny Quixote midget tilting at little windmills
to switch these channels off.

* that person the size of a thumb described in the Upanishads

Ubiquitous Voices of Boot, Panties, And...

What did they say? What did she hear
from the abandoned work boot in the road,
the stained and faded pink panties kicked
against the grimy door jamb downtown?
What did the scissors whisper from her purse,
the ones tucked there after the nurse used them
to remove sutures following surgery?

The boot, stiffened by heat, cold, rain and rays,
thumps against tires and scoots toward the edge
of the road, the ditch, as cars hit or clip its mouth
till it and its sole lie crumpled and mashed.
Was it abandoned because it did not fit some
tired and blistered foot? Was it tossed
from a window by a kid who could not know
the worth of twoness in love or shoes
when trudging hot asphalt or thorny paths?

And the panties, whose tattered will could
no longer hug elastic band to expanding
hips—what becomes of them?
Do they call to a gloved garbage collector
who stoops curious, then disgusted to scoop
them from their embarrassed place against
the green peeling door on Sixth Street?
Does he toss them into a bin or stinking mound
outside town, the way some folks cast
affection to the heap after heat?

And the scissors? What do they sliver
from within the woman's worn blue purse
after the nurse has snipped the stiff threads?
She will live a little longer now, half-a-woman,
but still...and at what cost...*at what cost,*
that thought suffocating almost
as much as the once-smothering lung.
Pray, some say; *meditate,* others advise.
But breathing hurts, she can't walk nor run,
and she won't lie to herself. At home,
she steadies her slow gait chair-to-chair
heading toward death's soon last air.

Punctuating Adrian

The strident urgency of my voice didn't match
the drone of what I was saying.
How *could* a comma after an introductory
adverbial clause matter as much as the lash
of wind's tongue against the window?

Or as much as the wrathful silence of Adrian's mom
at breakfast after his own voice had faltered,
halting to confess his no-choice.
She had defended him against his father's scorn,
his contempt for his disinterest in baseball or cars.
His early interest in dolls and clothes.

He muttered the truest words he'd ever uttered:
Mom, I'm...I'm gay...I've always known...uhm...
words trailing like a shadow in drag into silence,
stifled by clenched jaw, furrowed brow, and lips
pursed down into commas of disgust.

He begged her (as he had his small-town God)
to forgive him for his "sin,"...not to stop
loving him**, (See comma for short pause.)**
but she could not unknot the choke of scowl,
harder than the dry, half-eaten toast on her plate.

So Adrian did not know where he'd go
from that table, past this classroom, this site
of irrelevant rules behind stark walls.

"Commas mark brief pause**,**" I repeated.
Unlike scowls, he thought.
"If you use a period at the end of *dependent* thought**,
(note comma again)** *you create a* **fragment."**
Like me, he thought, as *the* **sentence** *runs on…
and on…and on.*

Lament for a Common Day

I.
Yesterday, I passed my chance to guzzle jazz
at the arboretum on a sun-dazzling Sunday.
I don't understand why I didn't go,
loving jazz as I do—
its freedom riffs and rides,
its saxaphonic slides, trumpeted yowls
dancing on chordal clouds,
dense, complex and blue as twilight.
Song coming on, trying to hold on
to that last sun-red glow stoked
by night's dark-blooded pulse.

II.
But instead of dervish-riding that tilt-a-twirl,
I stayed home.
I'd like to tell you that I rode cool sun down
slow and soft as a Ferris wheel till twilight,
where I watched November's Sweet-gum leaves
pale, gold, blush, and lisp toward Fall like me.

I'd like to report that I entered Sacred space—
humble, meditative, reflective—grateful
for resting nestled in grace of woods.

III.
But I can't say that either.
I did walk awhile, but oblivious to pine whispers
and foreshadowing shadows of cedars,
plaintive and mellow-dark as Sainte-Colombe's viol.

I read a bit, half-interested. I sat restless, listless.
I listened for Natural song—heard a crow's raw-nag call
and an unknown bird's persistent eeks squeaking
like Granny's rusting front porch swing.

Distant tires "wshhhhhhiii" on asphalt toward...
where or no-where really?

Evening: I fed cats, watched "Homeland,"
and *never* relaxed. I finished that day
unfinished, unsatisfied for the choice I'd made.

IV.
You must not judge me more harshly than I do.
I could have trodden a Sacred Way to Mysteries
from Athens to Eluesis, but Procrustes wooed me
from my path to his perfect bed.*
Once there, he found me too short,
so he stretched me upon his rack.
Then, my legs and my reach were too long,
so he chopped off my feet.

V.
Sun's jazz is gone.
Six o'clock's drizzle plips puddles dull-opal
and cedars cast deeper emerald-black regret.
Sainte-Colombe's bow moans.
No Indra's Net, these opals and emeralds do not,
do not reflect infinity.**
Hickory nuts pound the tin overhang,
sweet gum leaves stutter to the ground
fettered by rain heavy as Ophelia's skirts.***
Crows caw *haw-haw-haw* as the clock ticks.
Hooker moves in; delta blues descend,
and I sit unmoved, unsatisfied…unfinished….

*Procrustes invited guests to rest in his bed, then stretched or chopped them to fit the bed; **Indra's Web, Hindu god whose nets held jewels that reflected all jewels, all souls, all life; ***Hamlet's Ophelia, who drowned herself in despair.

PART II. PSYCHE ADMONISHES AND MURMURS

Witness

And a God of unknown origin and ragged persuasion
swept upon Nina again, convicting her mission
with a presence more menacing than stringent
smoke following her, more terrifying than the
Aye-aye* crouching on the edge of darkness, waiting
till the circle where she stooped and stared
into the fire flickered and smoldered into ash.

She knows the hungry eyes of the Aye-aye
determined toward the blackening blaze;
she hears the terrible ears twitch beyond
his rat face, and she accepts the Way
of long-pointed claws and sharp incisors.

Smoke and stench drench her will. She's tired.
Now, violet hope, like madras, bleeds to gray
after too many washes. She'd failed to stop
anything: beatings of Brother after he'd wet
and wept and prayed, the rape of a sister, leaned
yellow dressed, open-legged against the bus;
to stop that even after Bergen-Belsen. *Cleansing*
slaughters swept Poland, Bosnia, Darfur,
and oh…oh so much and no more!

She was no bodhisattva* dripping ambrosia to hell;
no Dalai Lama laughing, calling on kindness still.
Why hadn't she or the blessed Aye-aye already
gnawed the claws from Karadzic and her father?
Judgment rages now in the claw of a rat sniffing,
twitching, scratching in the bracken.

Nina's heart weighs a thousand, thousand pounds
of leaden nothing against a swallow's feather,
laid upon the scale.* And the Aye-aye waits.
Should she, like Jesus, who called for song
and dance after his Last Supper, rise and jig
before Golgotha, before the little Aye-aye
takes communion?

* 3-feet long rodent-like creature in Madagascar; *Buddhist teacher,
* Egyptian myth: a heart must weigh less than a feather to attain
immortality, escape being eaten by monster

Leaky Pen Whimpering in Sonora

I've come to this desert alone, wings folded
and clipped, tongue parched and dry,
belly growling, knowing only mirages of water;
the willow and cotton wood line the dry hole.

I've begged Calliope to come to me in Sonora,
my cup trembling, extended so empty,
I cannot even feed the two pigeons gurgling
beside me. The muse snores.

And though I grieve the prophetic stench of death
wafting the world from Myanmar, China, Iraq,
and I've heard the coming of the end, I cannot
find a vowel once I open my pouch, take out
my pad and pen. Words don't work anymore.

I've passed cactus lands of saguaro, ocotillo,
cholla, watched cat-claw's lemon-yellow blossoms
rise beside the juniper, despite the burning sand.
I've seen no water on my way to Mount Lemmon
where I sought respite from triple-digit heat.
And resting in her cool breath, I saw her twice-
charred pine. I grew mute again and blind.

And though this felt-tip Bic is bent and blunted.
leaking and splotching the page like blood,
I know where ink blots stop, freedom starts.

I will untie this tripping tongue to speak
the hearts of suffering ones, today, tomorrow—
no more whimpering from my desert, Sonora.

Komodo Dragon Meets Swollen Red Palm

In his dream, Ted growled a primal bellow
howling fury transcending time.
He attacked Komodo dragon, knowing
that *no matter how nice he was,* the beast
would devour him. So he leapt into air,
climbing walls, walking ceilings, ducking
flames, tail and claw, such supple speed,
he exhilarated triumph......till he woke.

Then he knew that standing defiant against
this foe who'd stalked his sleep for years
was not possible. Instead, he stood timid,
tentative, terrified! Stunted by too many
droughts of praise, too many silent scowls,
his thin skin split wide open, flesh rotting
sour as tomatoes on the vine, unable to hold
new growth after late summer rain.

Sometimes, he imagined charging the demon
like a wild boar. Yet, when he snorted, raising
tusks to attack, he felt mush-red, impotent
against one whose flaming tongue, lashing tail,
vicious claws, bared teeth always won.

And eleven wasps of the clock counted hours
that surrounded his stung and swollen palm;
fingers pointed out faults, ticking a bad end.
Thoughts panicked ostinato against death.
Insidious wordless accusations echoed
from childhood's silent cold house--
sissy, soft, unworthy...!

Other people saw Ted of this tale differently--
*sweet, sensitive, creative../*So he measured
all words against a kinder, larger clock,
not of wasps only, but the *now of true worth.*
He dowsed dragon's deadly venom,
banishing lethal labels to tongueless caverns.
Today, Ted sleeps tougher on a softer bed
where rhapsodic dreams ride lullabies.

Erosion Sighs and Cornbread Whines

Like the sandy red-clay hills where she lives,
she eroded by the how and how long she's lived.
Never tough enough, she barely survived
the loud, the lies, the loss.
Once-round jaws sag now, creviced and gullied,
set still determined to see spring.
In her submissive, unobtrusive way, she clings
to hope, stubborn as goat weed, clutching
the edge of Boo Gulch, dividing the pasture.

Hands, bruise-mapped as black-gum leaves in Fall,
still shell peas and shuck corn in summer and still
whip up pans of cornbread nightly. She strolls
ambered-oak, hickory-gold and star-lobed Sweetgum
paths, arboring October. Come November, she
makes cornbread dressing full of stock, sage and
gratitude for family, home for Thanksgiving. To her,
Kids, Fall and Cornbread are sacraments, *outward
and visible signs of inward and spiritual grace.* *

They'd been constant. She needs constancy now
that hickory nuts threaten her unsteady gait,
now that she feels earth tremor and quake
when she lies down, now that a fat angel sits
cross-legged watching from the window ledge.

She knows well that mosquitos will puncture
thin skin to live; she hears them buzz, sees them rise
from the mud-sludge beyond her window. That's why
she named her new stray cat, *Cornbread.* That's why
when he whines, *meowing,* imploring at the door,
she sighs, opens it wide and welcomes him in.
Think about it: there are 3 *other* seasons of Friend.

* Book of Common Prayer as cited in *Simple Abundance*, Nov. 9 *Sweet Surrender*

Sweet Surrender

Like a creature crawling the rim of her cup,
a shadow shifted, and Ruth halted, startled
before she sipped. Tricks of mind slip often
now, and she wondered if this were the way
good minds go into that black good yonder.

Ruth had been planted behind her window
too long, marveling only at natural miracles—
the return from Mexico of painted buntings,
the unlikely resurrections of petunias in June,
forgiveness from others for her imperfection.

May I go slowly, she prayed, *lingering here
a little longer to watch mischief grinning again
from my son's face as he conjures fantastic
stories, to see my daughters dwelling pregnant
and wild with life's meaningful possibilities.*

They comprehend, but she does not, the new
things like power point, Facebook, blogging,
twittering, split-second clickings of digital
miracles. In fact, she'd been phased out
and had felt her growing obsolescence.
*Some schools don't even put chalkboards
in classrooms anymore,* she thought.

She couldn't comprehend either, how greed
could disconnect *text* from context or heart
or separate Google from truth. Ruth could
not hide from what she did not know.

She did understand transience and tangled webs,
for she'd watched a brimming spring-fed pond
dry to a cloudy eye during drought. And she'd
built and burned three houses down herself.
She had *loved different people, knelt at
different graves, prayed at different altars.**
Still, she thought, amused at her halted sip,
*I'll take my leaving slow; I've always known
the peace that comes from no control.*

---

* Deepak Chopra, *The Spontaneous Fulfillment of Desire*, p.183

Seventy-Nine Days...

of no rain and no break till today. Myra called in sick.
Rain gurgles in gutters full of drought-curled leaves,
brittle twigs and spiders scurrying, inspecting
steely strands to reattach and catch multitudes
of moths, wasps, mosquitos, and droplets
hovering after rain, before and during
something called living.

As the rain hum-thrums against shingles and tin,
Myra welcomes a grayed-down, misty-mint aura
washing pastel across the day. She nestles into
her rocker grateful for the stop: *can't mow the lawn,
can't sweep the porch, can't walk the woods,
no need to water tomatoes nor beans.*

Out of French Roast coffee, she sips watery *stuff*
from a packet scooped into her bag after her last
stay at the La Quinta in Fort Worth.
Won't drive wet roads to Walmart today.
Weatherman forecasts rain for only one day.
No more constancy than that anyway, she sighs,
sinking deeper into her chair, sipping secret
respite from yesterday's labor and drought.

She'd dreamt badly the night before—
daughter, so sick she could not lift her arm,
and he, so gone, whispering his secrets
to someone beyond. *What wisdom
in uncertainty?* she wondered.

Tomorrow, when wildflowers, willful as she,
open wilder and brighter to sun, and grass sprigs
greener and more tender than brown-crackled ground,
she'd live the long list and worry about *ample* then:
gasoline, coffee, oatmeal, and eggs; a mop and
Dr. Scholl's, bills to pay, the Post Office….

But today, she'd talk to the rain:
Don't stop, she'd say; *and though your hum
subsides, soft splats keep time alive.*

PART III. PAST ECHOES

Synesthesia of Crystal's *Summer Time* Blues

Crystal's solo called up grief that I had known
like a sister in a warbling song-sparrow's song,
mysterious dark spot in the center of chest.
She housed her secret in the core of her breast,
marking silences, browner than the rest.
I wondered what shrouded her silence.

(One eye sees, the other senses.)

Crystal lifted her red-brown crown singing,
and her song trilled plaintive trebled notes
followed by deep, varied, sliding scales.

(As one ear hears, the other one knows.)

I knew that girl's "Summer Time" living
was no way easy, her tiny neck bordered by
heavy brown marks, alternating dark
and light stripes. But on stage, her dreams
took vocal-winged flight before
clouded eyes cleared.

My teacher-deaf ears could see, then,
melancholy of a songbird longing beyond
that brief perch to soar past huddling hovels
in the projects, bird-like versions of cup-like nests,
hidden and hushed amid concrete bracken
behind peeling walls and weed
beneath street light shadows.

(One mouth sings, the other one shuts.)

I heard yearning in a song sparrow's heart
trying to forget, learning to forgive
the mother who would not believe her,
the father who daily deceived her.
I had not…had not… even heard her
crystal clear calls, her amber soft voice,
lifting sorrow to the sky like a sparrow,
so tiny, so plain, so shy, so bright.

The Way of Cows

Daughter,
Do you recall that night you crawled
into bed with us when you heard Mama-Cinna,
penned in the barn bawling for Copper
after they'd been separated?

Her low moaning "noooooo" rose over and over
from the curved heavy sag of belly and her aching
full-bloated teat, her long tongue untouching
alfalfa heaped into her trough.

(Honey, I'm telling you what I knew then,
know now.)

Cinna's "Nooooooos" broke through the stall,
the corral, shattering my rest of the night.

And Copper panic-paced forth and back
thrusting his head through the slats toward
his mother's no-ing. His higher pitched "maaaaa"
"maaaaaa" went on all night.

I'll bet her great sad eyes tried, but could not
find one loose board nor hole to get to Copper
nor could they stop the dry-hay smell of dawn.

As we watched Bud cutting Copper from the crowd,
the cloud of dust stuck in our eyes, our nose...
our throats, and you just didn't get it—*September...
the drought...December.* Copper staggered
and entered the chute.

Honey, I've been up all night, and I'm hoarse
from bawling. We've got to find a hole
in this fence! Please call.
Love, Mom.

Unclasping Alice

Alice, a grinning, surreal effigy in baby blue dress,
black patent shoes and pure-white apron dangled
from a nail between two painted worlds.

One painting prismed pastel light within
a greenhouse; panes cut lines and designs,
elaborate, varied and complicated as life.
Emeralds, aquas and mauves cubed and implored
toward a latch, a rainbow, an aria
beyond the hothouse door.

But mom and the Alice-doll hung suspended
between that door and Georgia's *Music,* roiling
waves swelling long celloed phrases of sorrow,
layered and lifting from a blue cerulean center.
Pale magenta erupts into time's titanium bubble.

And though the woman watched her Alice
hang helpless between bubble and door,
she couldn't lift her from the nail of her cross.
Alice had crawled down too many holes
after too many elusive rabbits and hatters.
Courage shatters after so many empty holes.

So, the mother rocked wet-towel limp, lamenting,
staring into fear and loss. She could not unlock
the clasp, nor rise above purple-muffled sobs.
All she could do was pray untongued alone.

And after forty proverbial nights, she saw light
slide across the room to the wall, saw the wall
shift, saw Alice's eyes turn left, then right.
Her tiny hand stretched space to touch the rim
of a sunlit frame. By grace, she clasped
and lifted that emerald greenhouse latch.

Mama Rasps *Help* as Queen of the Night Inherits

The black-shadowed leaf lifted from the log
and waved thin-fingered and unsteady
as Mother's left-handed reluctant goodbye
quivered from her thin-bodied bed.
Steel-bellied truth stares me down on days
like today; cold, cloudy as brittle leaves laugh.
Lemon Lysol strives to drive dying smells
into corners, but caving belly and eyes
whisper gardenia wreaths while the orderly's mop
swishes and slicks the speckled tile, yet misses
one black drop beneath the metallic porta-pot.
Dr. Pennaclear promised peace here
at Westwood Place; Dr. Pennaclear lied.

Yet Here was inevitable, for everyone was busy—
I had papers to grade, Sis had insurance to sell,
Bud had the bush hog to hook up,
and Dad had the home-health nurse to screw
in the back room of our home
as Mama lay rasping "Help," barely breathing
from the bed she'd shared with him for 54 years.
So…we reap what we sow, some say,
and when the cat dies away, the rat will play.

Into that long day's journey into night,
wild arms flailed sheets from her fevered flesh,
and in her first-ever nakedness, shrill laughter
shattered thin-walled silence, startling
a porcelain Madonna from the edge of a ledge.
I bent to scoop the uprooted ivy,
but instead, woke my father, whose dozing head
slumped in his ever slumber, to scoop the roots
and undone dirt, to wipe without will such spots
beneath my mother's bed.

Finally I, Queen of one Night, sat unafraid
and upright upon my mother's throne;
I inherited; now, I shall not inherit!
Lavender morning comes, and everything works
if you don't think about it.
The sugar water sack sags, so few drops left;
outside, the wind gusts purple,
and a leaf lifts to curl like a fist.

Nonc Jules and Lachez-Les*

As Merlin Fontenot dragged his bow,
fiddling fast then slow to call joy up
and call work down that Saturday night
at Hampton's honky tonk where woe
rests from the week and feet take
a turn at the "Lachez-les Two Step,"
Nonc Jules conjured spells daring
Douzat to squeeze his accordion,
calling "eh-hah's" and "oh-yeahs,"
pulsing longings for women and whiskey
by night and Yvonne's black coffee
by day, to drink and dance and laugh,
lewd and loud, before next mass.

Jules tapped his foot to the band:
one-and-two step; one-and-two step.

Then, the sway-backed man waltzed in—
wiry, thin, stubbled toothless chin.
Khaki clad, grease smeared across
one shoulder where he'd lain beneath
some old wreck or gumbo-caked tractor
(or more likely) where he'd curled
fetal, wine-dizzy toward demi-sleep.

His slight feet kept the beat as he
slid onto the floor, one-and-two step,
one-and-two stomp, winding among those
who made way for the man who closed
his eyes to them, who opened only to

song—"Guidry's Two-Step," one-and-two
touch, one-and-two stomp, or "Pelican's
Waltz: ONE-two-three, ONE-two-three.
Grinning, he danced blind to time.

Me? I could not budge from my chair.
Shadowed by a post that kept the ceiling
from falling, I wanted to die, to hide
from the side-wise smiles of those who
shrugged my Papa, shuffling unabashed
to the zydeco grate of the rub-board,
nodding the throb of the base and drum.

One-and-two step, one-and-two stomp.
Oh, I burned. I yearned, too, to take
Papa's rough dark hand in mine, and say,
"Please, lead me, Papa, to lachez-les."

*Nonc Jules and Lachez-Les, Trans. "Uncle Jules and Let-it-be", a band playing at a Cajun Folk Festival, Nachitoches, LA, 1997

Not Sure Why I'm Confiding,

but take my hand anyway,...come with me
to the warm room of the red glow
that opened ecstasy
and closed confusion
for a brief while.
Intervals in a small space.

There was a great warm hand
that laid across my pelvis, then,
fingertips that moved slowly
at first...then fervently,
passion that drew fluid tremors toward yes
till hips thrust and writhed in a rhythm
that begged to be met,
begged to be filled,
begged to prolong ecstasy,
to feel, to feel...to feel forever-
fevered seconds that last
beyond anything, everything:
the room, the past...tomorrow.

And when feeling could no longer hold
infra-red, it would blaze white hot light
for mystical, infinite seconds...
to subside finally into amber-soft
embers of after...
eddies of love (or not love).

But inevitable blue weathers of world
hurled hand and pelvis from the room
against the sea wall of real,
scattering passion's liminal ash
to float and sink its earnest, ephemeral seed.

The red room emptied of bed, pelvis, hand.
Today, stark-cold January sun crawls
shadows across blonde-smudged carpet.

Did it matter? Was it numinous? Does it last
beyond moment and room?
Are these the right questions?

Spoonful of Vanity; Year Full of Vision

Before the gala, she draped her smalling self
shimmery gold, slinking folds softly over
the scar tracking its long way down, down.
She'd quaffed Clairoled hair by heated wand
and brushed a blush upon her cheek, up, up.

At the gala, they said she looked *lovely...great!*
They did not say...*for one who's been around
the bend* of life and death and back again.
She had hidden their eyes from what she'd seen
of pain and dread of slow death.

After the gala, she stripped the lying silk,
gazed upon her naked self,
appalled by the truth etched before her.
She slipped into sweats instead of the starched,
creased jeans stretched across the bed.

She would wear looser clothes.
She had already grown more aware of threats
like hands and handles, brown air and water,
the *what* she ate, the *where* she went,
the *whom* she loved, the *how* she said,

the *if* she did, the *when* she quit...
the *why,* the *why...*the *is* of things
like violence, war, disease, and surgeons
who nick the phrenic nerve of breath,
the breadth of life, her will to live.

PART IV. WOODS WHISPER

Restless Heart Hears and Asks...

how paradox chops legs off comprehension,
how anxiety rides the slow loping back of peace?
Natural prompts ask, too, as birds flute sweet
incessant longings in thousand-pitched tones.
Orioles flap hunger to jam-dolloped platters,
and crows call, call, cousins to cast off crumbs.
A ruby-throated hummer helicopters salvia,
that same bird, perhaps, who stabbed the breast
and stopped the song of a mockingbird.
(I pulled his fierce beak free to set him free.)

A gun shot pierces morning with its lethal hole.
A motorboat growls and churns distant waters,
and a weed eater whines and sputters as it shreds
dandelions, red clover, and pepper grass to scents.
From this fresh ether of grass, ugly words intrude,
offend—*vetch, yucca, buzzard, bastard cabbage....*

A neighbor calls Meg to breakfast.
Cardinals lilt and warble; Jays yap.
Hedonically, we adapt
as music and noise ride hammer and anvil side by side.
No longer muddled, I guzzle flux,
devouring every morseled sound with *a vibrant ache
that under-rides being*...being alive.

I tell you, I do *not* fear death,
the loss of voice, *that* long silence.
But I'm terrified of the deafened ear,
the hushed voice of love that would come
from losing you.

To Bark, Who Speaks a Handful

Strip of bark, width and length
of a small woman's hand,
sleight-of-life fallen from a great dead tree,
long diseased, I listen slowly, study closely

your dry-fractaled bark, ash-dark
and ounces light. I turn you palm-up,
and a mere one-half inch beneath reptilian skin,
I trace your under-bark, once sap-moist part

that clung to the trunk for so long
before you finally let go.
There, wood-pulp streaks vertical rivulets
dry-flowing toward a fall

off ragged edges.
They stop abruptly like one who halts
startled by the next step—
upon a snake, into a hole, over a cliff.

One dry haired tendril of sap still clings
to the creviced underbelly of bark.
And two holes portal sun's light now:
was it here that insects and death bored?

One worm-like curl tried to unwind itself
as if deciding not to stay, but did.
It breaks the linear path, the pattern, the way
extreme heat, wind, freeze, disease—shatters,

disrupts, or delays life's rhythmic plan.
Whatever it was, this hull of life—
this piece of a thing—does it equal
the sum of its parts? Its whole?

All I know is this:
this too slight width and length of bark,
the size of a small woman's hand, is all—
all I have left…of you.

"A Bird in the Hand..."

She wants to cup her hand around the quickened
heart of one chickadee, to wrap his smallness,
his wildness, his beauty in the darkened dome
of her palm. No need to keep him from anything—
foraging, flight, freedom, song. She just wanted
to enfold and finger his sharp perfection—
twiggy feet, nervous beak, black-capped head,
shades of grays, pure whites clearly defined
from behind glass at a distance.

She wanted to stroke wings that mount
and swim sky without worry or doubt.
She'd watched chickadees for years,
the way they'd perch and wait and wait
as titmice, cardinals, and finches fluttered
flapped and pecked about feeders, crowding
out small ones who swooped and smart-darted
among the larger ones for the quick steal.

She wonders, though, what dark impulse
prompts her to *want* to capture,
to hold for an instant such an innocent.
She remembers eye-darting, heart-thumping
helplessness and wonders
what link sleazes between urge and act,
between lust and clutch?
What good comes from a touch
that costs one helpless second of terror?

Just a Dove's Worth

Why, just this morning, a dove, drab gray,
waded slowly into my bird-bath to sip water
and dip vague-marked wings into coolness.
When he'd drunk and bathed enough, he spread
webbed wings, vibrant Vinca-red, and flew away.
I'd never seen his brilliance till today.

Back home, folks used to wade importantly
into Clear Springs, arms crossed across hearts
believing those waters would wash away shame.
The difference between dove and men being—
the dove never doubted his beauty nor worth.

Sad Heart, what are you trying to prove?
How deeply must you frack this earth
before you hit shale and the fuel of worth?
How many worms, sticky pale, eating dirt,
must you meet on your way down before
you know you deserve to live above muck?
How high must you climb before you learn
how thin the air can be, how brief the season,
how wildflowers dwarf at the top?

Stop that black hairy-tongued reaction*
before frustration's blue tantrum destroys us.
Lift and flap your arms like the once-wings
they were when you were born. Dredge words
that stunted and tainted goodness in a murky-
watered past, drag them to shore, and torch them.
Finger their cold ashes with forgiveness,
Any single thing (word act job...)
and scatter them helpless to hurt another.

Any single one (mom man god...)
that does not bring you alive
is too small for you. *

*Black hairy tongue, reaction to penicillin; * Mark Nepo, *The Book of Awakening*

So Confused, Said the Squirrel

Though my jaws recede, my overbite weak-seeming,
I crack the hardest hickory nuts for meager meat
and shred thorniest cones for tiny seed.
I climb flimsy, spindly twigs balancing
life with a swish of my full-fluff tail.
I leap two, no three, feet to the next tree.

I've clawed my way up greased steel rails
for food meant only for cardinals and chickadees.
I've chewed through wood and plastic
to survive triple-digit heat, single-digit cold.
I've clutched and stretched from pole to pole,
hanging upside down for sunflower seeds.

I've dodged bullets, pellets, and rocks.
To some, I'm a rodent, a thief, a pest.
To others, I'm a meal or a marvel.
To a few, I'm a pet. For years I rode shoulders
of a man who tucked peanuts in a pocket.
For another, I scampered eleven steps to the click
of two pecans, snatched one and scurried down.

Some creatures *baffle* me; they give up easily,
retreating behind glass in January and July,
watching us whish from limb to flimsy limb
with more will and grace than they
who study our ways.

I don't get it!
I've hung *upside down* for life,
descending head-first to earth, eyes wide open,
tail swishing faith in fickle air
and the thud of a fallen acorn.

Spotted Bee Balm Soothes Parched Pasture

Everywhere I think today, I hear love's adagio.
Especially when I gaze upon clusters
of Monarda Punctata, Spotted Bee Balm,
rising like purple pagodas, spirit-scenting
promised whispers of healing amid pastures,
barren after long drought.

My first breath of its tender touch crawled
Palo Duro's canyon walls many struggles ago.
Today, I remember tenderness.

I know how Bee balm lowers fever,
relieves cough, soothes sting and burn of skin.
I know how it draws swallowtail butterflies,
hummingbirds, and me to the templed garden
where love strums forgotten beauties:

--The palm of a 3-year-old cradling my face,
her old friend, whose eyes focus then
on the heart of what's said, what's true.

--Mom's bruise-mapped arm lapped over Dad's
as both watch Gulf's sunset ride tides
dappling, rising, subsiding....

--A great warm hand squeezing courage
to this trembling cold one before I turn
the knob to work one February more.

--Fingertips transforming "Un" to beautiful
when a lover traced the curve of my hip
as if it were the lip of God.

Today, Pagoda flowers lift my dry now
by stirring breezes of other thens,
wild-planted in the tender speechless real.

ACKNOWLEDGMENTS

I'm grateful to the following publications where these poems first appeared. They are arranged in the order of their appearance in this manuscript except where multiple poems appeared in the same publication.

"Witness," *Writing Texas*, (Texas Association of Creative Writing Teachers Journal, published by Lamar University Press), 2014

"Leaky Pen Whimpering in Sonora," *Book of the Year,"* (Anthology of state first place Awards by Poetry Society of Texas) 2013

"Sweet Surrender," *Book of the Year,* (Poetry Society of Texas) 2011

"Synesthesia of Crystal's Summer Time Blues," published as "One Ear Hears, The Other One Feels" in *Book of the Year,* (Poetry Society of Texas) 2006

"The Way of Cows," *Book of the Year,* (Poetry Society of Texas) 2013

"Nonc Jules and Lachez-Les," *The Mochila Review* (published by Missouri Western State College) 2003

"A Bird in the Hand…," *Her Texas,* forthcoming from Wings Press, 2014

After completing her Ph.D. from L.S.U., Charlotte Renk settled in Athens, Texas to teach English and Creative Writing. For thirty years, she has written poetry and short stories inspired by natural settings and local folk surrounding life in her small cabin nestled among tall pine woods, hickories, oaks, and wildflowers of East Texas. Eakin Press published her prizewinning collection of poetry, *THESE HOLY HUNGERS: SECRET YEARNINGS FROM AN EMPTY CUP,* 2009, and Poetry in the Arts published her book, *SOLIDAGO, AN ALTAR TO WEEDS,* 2010. She has published in such journals as *Kalliope, Mochila Review, New Texas, Concho River Review, Sow's Ear, Langdon Review of the Arts in Texas, Re: Arts and Letters,* and *Southwest Review*. She received the National Storyteller Award for fiction. Still writing, publishing, and conducting workshops on writing, she explores certain recurring subjects: love (from passion to compassion), family, loss, natural settings, teaching, and hiking.

49

www.ingramcontent.com/pod-product-compliance
Lightning Source LLC
Chambersburg PA
CBHW072036060426
42449CB00010BA/2285